A Picture Book of

WILD CATS

Written by Mary Scott
Illustrated by Roseanna Pistolesi

Troll Associates

SERVAL

Big ears and long legs. Those are the parts of a serval's body that you notice right away. This cat's ears help it listen for small animals and lizards. And its long legs help it run very fast to catch these animals. Servals can also jump very high, and they are good climbers. This helps them catch birds and other animals that live in trees.

Servals live in Africa. They like to lie in the long grass during the hot day. At night, it is time to hunt.

Library of Congress Cataloging-in-Publication Data

Scott, Mary, (date)
   A picture book of wild cats / by Mary Scott; illustrated by
Roseanna Pistolesi.
      p.   cm.
   Summary: Describes the appearance, habits, and habitat of several
wild cats, including the mountain lion, cheetah, and ocelot.
   ISBN 0-8167-2430-X (lib. bdg.)   ISBN 0-8167-2431-8 (pbk.)
   1. Felidae—Juvenile literature.   [1. Felidae.   2. Cats.]
I. Pistolesi, Roseanna, ill.   II. Title.
QL737.C23S42   1992
599.74'428—dc20   91-16500

Printed in the United States of America.
10 9 8 7 6 5 4 3

MOUNTAIN LION

This big cat has lots of different names. It is also called a puma, a cougar, a panther, or a catamount. But whatever you call it, this is one of the largest cats in North and South America.

Mountain lions usually hunt at night. They use their sharp eyes and good sense of smell to find food. Deer and elk are their favorite meals, but a mountain lion will eat smaller animals and birds, too.

JAGUAR

The jaguar is the biggest cat in North and South America. They can be up to eight and a half feet (2.6 meters) long and weigh 300 pounds (135 kilograms). But jaguars weigh only two pounds (.9 kilogram) when they are born. They stay with their mother for about two years, learning how to hunt deer, wild pigs, rodents, fish, turtles, and other animals.

INDIAN TIGER

A tiger's stripes do more than make it look beautiful. They also help the tiger hide in the long grass, so it can sneak up on its prey. Stripes also help us tell one tiger from another. No two tigers have the same pattern of stripes.

Tigers like to be by themselves. The only tigers that live together are a mother and her *cubs*, or babies. A tiger usually has 2–4 cubs. The cubs start learning how to hunt when they are about six months old. But they will stay with their mother for several years.

Although most cats don't like water, tigers love it. A swim is a great way to keep cool and get away from annoying insects. And splashing and playing in the water is lots of fun!

LION

Lions spend about twenty hours a day resting. But when night falls, lions begin to hunt. Lions like to hunt at night because it is easier for them to sneak up on their prey in the dark. A lion can't run very fast, so it must catch its dinner by surprise. It creeps through the long grass very quietly. When the lion is close to the animal it is stalking, it runs forward and grabs it.

Unlike most cats, lions like to be with one another. They live together in groups called *prides*. A pride is a family group that includes several adult males, adult females (called *lionesses*), and a number of young cubs. Male cubs stay with a pride until they are two or three years old. Then the adults chase them away. In time, the young lions will be strong enough to lead prides of their own.

LEOPARD

A tree is a leopard's favorite place. It likes to sleep
stretched out on a branch. A leopard even climbs
through the branches when it is hunting. And if a
leopard jumps down to kill a deer or another large
animal, it drags its food into a tree to eat it. A leopard
has to be very strong to do this!

The *black panther* is really just a leopard with a black coat.
They have the same black spots as leopards do—the spots are
just hard to see under the animal's black fur. A black kitten
may be born in the same group, or *litter*, as normal-colored kittens.

CARACAL

It's easy to recognize a caracal—
just look at its ears! Tufts of long black
hair grow from the tips of this cat's ears.
Although it is not as big as other wild cats—
a caracal is only about two and a half feet (.76 meter)
long—this cat is a fierce hunter. Its favorite food is
birds. Caracals like to hunt at night, because that is
when birds rest in the trees. A caracal can even kill an eagle!

BOBCAT

This North American cat got its name from its short, or *bobbed*, tail. It can live almost anyplace, from woods to swamps to deserts. Bobcats will even live on the edges of towns! But they are so good at hiding that you aren't likely to see one.

A bobcat can hear and see very well, and it is a very good hunter. Small animals, such as rabbits, squirrels, mice, and birds, are its favorite foods.

CHEETAH

When a cheetah is standing still, its legs seem to be too long for its body. But a cheetah looks very beautiful when it is running. Those long legs help the cheetah run faster than any other animal—up to seventy miles (110 kilometers) an hour! This lets a cheetah catch antelope and other animals.

Cheetahs make many different sounds. They growl, snarl, mew, and purr, and even produce a birdlike chirp!

A female cheetah gives birth to 2–4 cubs, but many cubs are killed by hyenas, lions, and leopards. If a cub does survive, it will stay with its mother for about fifteen months. It has a lot to learn to become as good a hunter as Mom!

MARGAY

Not much is known about this wild cat, which lives in Mexico and South America. It has large eyes, which scientists think help it hunt at night. Margays may like to eat rats, mice, rabbits, and birds.

JAGUARUNDI

This cat's name sounds like "jaguar," but the jaguarundi doesn't look like a jaguar at all. In fact, its head looks more like a weasel's than a cat's. Small for a wild cat—it is only three or four feet (.91–1.2 meters) long and weighs about twenty pounds (9 kilograms)—the jaguarundi hunts for mice, rats, and birds during the day or night. Like many cats, the jaguarundi likes to be by itself as it roams through its home in the southwestern United States and South America.

CLOUDED LEOPARD

The clouded leopard, on the right side of this picture, lives in the hot, wet jungle of southern Asia. The clouded leopard spends most of its time in trees, and catches its dinner by jumping down on small animals, monkeys, and wild pigs.

SNOW LEOPARD

Not many people have seen the beautiful snow leopard, shown on the left. This shy cat lives high in the mountains of Asia, in a lonely world of snow and rocks. Its long, thick fur helps the snow leopard keep warm in its cold home. Thick hair on its big paws lets the cat walk easily on the snow, and keeps its feet warm, too! The snow leopard sleeps all day, then wakes up at night to hunt for goats, sheep, deer, and rabbits.

SIBERIAN TIGER

This big cat looks a lot like its close relative, the Indian tiger, but there are a few differences between them. Because the Siberian tiger lives where it is cold, its coat is very thick. Its fur is also a lighter color than the Indian's. This helps the Siberian tiger hide against the snow and ice as it creeps up on the sheep, buffalo, and other large animals it likes to eat.

Tigers are the largest of all cats. An adult male can weigh more than 420 pounds (189 kilograms) and is over nine feet (2.7 meters) long. Its tail alone is three feet (.91 meter) long! It takes a lot of food to keep such a big body going. A tiger can eat more than fifty pounds (22.5 kilograms) of meat in one night!

PALLAS'S CAT

    This little cat lives high in the mountains of Asia. Its silver fur helps it blend in with the snow. Long fur on the bottom of its body helps the cat keep warm when it lies on snow-covered ground. And the Pallas's cat's big eyes help it see the mice and other small animals it likes to hunt.

EUROPEAN WILDCAT

You may think this animal looks like a pet cat you might have at home, but the wildcat really *is* wild. It is very hard to tame and cannot be kept as a pet.

This cat once lived all over Europe and Asia. Now it is found only in northern Scotland and other remote places in Europe. Not much is known about the wildcat. It is active mainly at night, so most people never see one.

OCELOT

Climbing trees is a favorite sport for this cat, which lives in South America and parts of the southwestern United States. Moving quickly through the branches at night, the ocelot hunts for monkeys, porcupines, lizards, birds, and mice.

The ocelot is sometimes called the ''leopard cat'' or ''tiger cat.'' In spite of these fierce nicknames, the ocelot is usually a playful and gentle animal. And it is one of the most beautiful of all the wild cats.